SEARCH for LIBERATION

BOOKS by

His Divine Grace

A.C. Bhaktivedanta Swami Prabhupāda

published by *Krishna Books Inc*

Bhagavad-gītā As It Is
Śrīmad Bhāgavatam (30 volume set)
Śrī Caitanya-caritāmṛta (17 volume set)
Kṛṣṇa, the Supreme Personality of Godhead
Teachings of Lord Chaitanya
Teachings of Queen Kuntī
Śrī Īśopaniṣad
The Nectar of Devotion
The Science of Self-Realization
Rāja-vidyā: The King of Knowledge
Easy Journey to Other Planets
Kṛṣṇa, the Reservoir of Pleasure
The Perfection of Yoga
Beyond Birth and Death
On Chanting Hare Kṛṣṇa
Life Comes From Life
The Path of Perfection
Perfect Questions, Perfect Answers
Search for Liberation

SEARCH for LIBERATION

Featuring
a conversation between

JOHN LENNON

and

A.C. BHAKTIVEDANTA
SWAMI PRABHUPĀDA

FOUNDER-ĀCĀRYA OF THE INTERNATIONAL SOCIETY FOR KRISHNA CONSCIOUSNESS

Search for Liberation

Krishna Books Inc is licensed by the
Bhaktivedanta Book Trust
to print and publish the literary works of

His Divine Grace
A. C. Bhaktivedanta Swami Prabhupāda

Readers interested in obtaining other titles by the author may contact Krishna Books Inc:

www.krishnabooks.org
or email: info@krishnabooks.org

Library of Congress Catalog Card Number: 81-66041
Original ISBN: 0-89213-109-8

KBI Reprint 2015

Printed and bound by Thomson Press (India) Ltd.

CONTENTS

INTRODUCTION

On a cold December night in 1966, an elderly Indian Swami climbed into a Volkswagen van with about fifteen of his followers and their instruments (including a harmonium loaned by Allen Ginsberg) and drove uptown to a recording studio near Times Square. They weren't professional musicians, but in a few hours they'd recorded an LP that even the producer was excited about. It was a special album, more than just music. It was chanting and meditation; it was worship. A few months laver a letter arrived at a small storefront temple on New York's Lower East Side. Someone had heard the album and told the Beatles about it. They ordered one hundred copies.

George Harrison would later recall in a November 1980 interview the impression Śrīla Prabhupāda's album, *Krishna Consciousness,** made on them. "I remember singing it [the Hare Kṛṣṇa *mantra*]. Just for days, John and I, with ukulele banjos, sailing through the Greek islands—Hare Kṛṣṇa. Like six hours we sang, because you couldn't stop once you got going. You just couldn't stop. It was like as soon as you stop, it was like the lights went out."

In September 1969, Śrīla Prabhupāda, the founder of the Hare Kṛṣṇa movement, arrived as a house guest at Tittenhurst Park, the beautiful eighty acre British estate owned by John Lennon. Three or four times a week Śrīla Prabhupāda gave public lectures in a tall, stately building at the northern end of the property a hundred yards from the main house, in which John and Yoko lived.

The building had been formerly used as a hall for chamber music recitals, but now several of Śrīla Prabhupāda's disciples, who resided along with him in a block of guest houses on the property, installed a small Deity altar and a podium for Śrīla Prabhupāda. The building never really had a name, but after Śrīla Prabhupāda's arrival, everyone called it "the Temple."

They still call it "the Temple" today, and except for the recent addition of an enormous crimson-and-gold pipe organ

---

*1976 Happening Records, New York

nearly covering the towering west wall, it exists unchanged, now surrounded by a recording studio complex owned by Ringo Starr.

Nineteen sixty-nine was for John Lennon a year of intense search for social and personal liberation. He had already been to the Maharishi and later would enter primal therapy and left-wing politics. He was in a major transitional period; he had married Yoko Ono in March, and the Beatles were about to break up.

On September 14, John, Yoko, and George Harrison, after enjoying an Indian vegetarian meal prepared by the devotees at the Temple, walked over to Śrīla Prabhupāda's quarters for their first meeting. Three months before in Montreal, some of the Hare Kṛṣṇa devotees had sung with John and Yoko during the recording of "Give Peace a Chance." And now they were about to meet the *guru* who brought the Hare Kṛṣṇa *mantra* to the West.

Their lively discussion with Śrīla Prabhupāda, which constitutes the major portion of this book, deals with the path to peace and liberation, the eternality of the soul, reincarnation, the nature of God, qualifications of the *guru,* and the authority of *Bhagavad-gītā* (the Indian spiritual classic still sacred to 600 million people).

In a conversation sometimes lightly humorous, sometimes intense, the reader will be struck by Śrīla Prabhupāda's prophetic use of President Kennedy's assassination to dramatize the temporality of human life and how the soul lives on after death, subjects that John would explore in his later songs. Explaining that John should have nothing to fear either in life or death, Śrīla Prabhupāda declares:

> "When this body ceases to exist, you will continue to exist... The soul is eternal and the body is temporary... But that minute quantity of the Absolute within us [the soul] is very great when compared to material knowledge. Material knowledge is practically no knowledge whatsoever. It is covered knowledge. But when one is liberated and attains liberated knowledge, his knowledge is very much greater than the greatest material knowledge."

SEARCH FOR LIBERATION

A Conversation Between
John Lennon and Swami Bhaktivedanta

Śrīla Prabhupāda [to John Lennon]: You are anxious to bring about peace in the world. I've read some of your statements, and they show me that you're anxious to do something. Actually, every saintly person should be anxious to bring peace to the world. But we must know the process. In *Bhagavad-gītā* [5.29], Lord Kṛṣṇa explains how to achieve peace: "The sages, knowing Me as the ultimate purpose of all sacrifices and austerities, the Supreme Lord of all planets and demigods, and the benefactor and well-wisher of all living entities, attain peace from the pangs of material miseries."

People can become peaceful by knowing three things. If people perfectly understand only these three things, then they'll become peaceful. What are they? First of all, Lord Kṛṣṇa says that He is the real enjoyer of all the sacrifices, austerities, and penances that people undertake to perfect their lives. For instance, your own musical activities are also a form of austerity. Your songs have become popular because you have undergone some austerities. You have come to perfection, but that required some penances and austerities. Scientific discoveries also require austerities. In fact, anything valuable requires austerity. If one works very devoutly and painstakingly, one becomes successful.

That is called *yajña* or sacrifice. It is also called *tapasya,* or penance. So Kṛṣṇa says that He is the enjoyer of the results of your *tapasya*. He claims, "The result of your *tapasya* should come to Me. Then you'll be satisfied."

The second thing people should remember is that Kṛṣṇa is the supreme proprietor. People are claiming, "This is my England," "This is my India," "This is my Germany," "This is my China." No! Everything belongs to God, Kṛṣṇa. Not only this planet belongs to Kṛṣṇa, but all other planets in the universe.

Still, we have divided even this planet into so many nations. Originally, this planet was not divided. From the historical accounts in the *Mahābhārata,* we understand that the whole planet was once ruled by a single emperor who resided in India, in the place called Hastināpura, the site of modern Delhi. Even up to five thousand years ago there was only one king, Maharaja Pariksit. The whole planet was under one flag and was called Bhārata-varṣa. But gradually Bhārata-varṣa has become smaller and smaller and smaller. For instance, very recently, just twenty years ago, the remaining portion of Bhārata-varṣa, now called India, was divided into Pakistan and Hindustan. Actually, India was one, but now it has been reduced by the partition. This dividing is going on.

The Earth Is God's Place

But actually this whole planet is God's place. It's nobody else's place. How can we claim possession? For example, you have given me this place to stay in. If I stay for one week and then claim, "Oh, this is my room," is that a very nice thing? There will immediately be some disagreement, some trouble. Rather, I should recognize the actual fact, namely, that you have kindly spared this room. By your permission I'm living here, comfortably. And when it is necessary for me to leave, I shall go.

Similarly, we all come here into the kingdom of God empty-handed, and we go empty-handed. So how can I claim that this is my property, this is my country, this is my world, this is my planet? Why do we make such claims? Is it not insanity? So Lord Kṛṣṇa says, *sarva-loka-maheśvaram:* "I am the Supreme Lord of every place."

Thirdly, we should always remember that Kṛṣṇa is the real friend of every living entity and that He is sitting as a friend within everyone's heart. He's such a nice friend. In this material world, we make friendships, but they break up. Or my friend lives somewhere, and I live somewhere else. But Kṛṣṇa is such a nice friend that He is living within—within me and within my heart. He is the best friend of all living beings. He's not just the friend of a select few, but is dwelling even within the heart of the most insignificant creature as Paramātma, or Supersoul.

The Peace Formula

So if these three things are understood clearly, then one becomes peaceful. This is the real peace formula. Everything is there in *Bhagavad-gītā*. One simply has to study it. Just like arithmetic—there are so many types of mathematical calculations, such as addition, subtraction, multiplication, division, and fractions. One has to learn them by careful study. So *Bhagavad-gītā* is the best book to study for learning the spiritual science.

But please don't think that it's simply because I am preaching Kṛṣṇa consciousness that I am advocating *Bhagavad-gītā*. No. It is accepted by scholars and theologians not only in India but all over the world. Perhaps you already know this, but there are thousands of *Bhagavad-gītā* translations in English, French, German—all languages.

Even scholarly Mohammedans read *Bhagavad-gītā*. I know one Mohammedan professor in India who was a great devotee of Lord Kṛṣṇa. He did not openly disclose that he was a devotee, but each year he observed Kṛṣṇa's appearance day, Janmastami, by fasting and writing an article about Kṛṣṇa. He and many other Mohammedans read *Bhagavad-gītā*.

And when I was a young man in Calcutta, an Englishman was a tenant in the house of one of my friends. So when this Englishman was vacating the house, we went to take possession of his quarters, and we saw that he had many books, including a copy of *Bhagavad-gītā*. My friend, Mr. Mullik, was a little astonished that this Englishman, a Christian, had a copy of *Bhagavad-gītā*. Mr. Mullik was touching the book, causing the Englishman to suspect that he was going to be asked to part with it. So the Englishman immediately said. "Oh, Mr. Mullik, I cannot present that book to you. It is my life and soul."

Bhagavad-gītā is accepted by scholars and philosophers of all nationalities. Therefore, I think people should have one scripture, one God, one *mantra,* and one activity: one God, Kṛṣṇa; one scripture, *Bhagavad-gītā;* one *mantra,* Hare Kṛṣṇa; and one activity, to serve Kṛṣṇa. Then there will actually be peace all over the world. I request you to at least try to understand this philosophy to your best ability. And if you think that it is valuable, then please take it up. You want to give something to the world. So why not give them Kṛṣṇa consciousness?

The Lord says, "Whatever action is performed by a great man, common men follow in his footsteps. And whatever standards he sets by exemplary acts, all the world pursues." [Bg. 3.21] The idea is that if something is accepted by the leading persons, the ordinary persons follow. If the leading person says it is all right, then others also accept it. So by the grace of God, Kṛṣṇa, you are leaders. Thousands of young people follow you. They like you. And if you give them something actually spiritual, the face of the world will change.

The Kṛṣṇa consciousness movement is not newly manufactured. From the historical point of view, it is at least five thousand years old. The *Bhagavad-gītā,* which is the basis of Kṛṣṇa consciousness, was spoken by Lord Kṛṣṇa five thousand years ago. Of course, the *Gītā* is generally regarded as an Indian religious book. But it isn't—it's not simply Indian or Hindu. The *Bhagavad-gītā* is meant for all people of the world, and not even just for human beings but for all other living creatures as well. In Chapter 14 the Lord says, "It should be understood that all species of life, O son of Kuntī, are made possible by birth in this material nature and that I am the seed-giving father." [Bg. 14.4]

This indicates that the eternal living entity appears in varieties of temporary, material forms, just like we here now have the forms of ladies, gentlemen, and young men. We all have different forms. This whole world is full of varieties of life, but Kṛṣṇa says, *aham bīja-pradaḥ pitā:* "I am the father of all of them." *Pitā* means "father." So the Lord claims all living entities as His sons.

Beyond Sectarianism

Some people may say that Kṛṣṇa is Indian, Kṛṣṇa is Hindu, or Kṛṣṇa is something else. But, no—Kṛṣṇa is actually the Supreme Personality of Godhead, the seed-giving father of all living things on this planet. This Kṛṣṇa consciousness movement was started by Kṛṣṇa Himself. Therefore, it isn't sectarian; it's meant for everyone.

And in *Bhagavad-gītā* [9.34l, Kṛṣṇa describes the universal process for worshipping Him:

man-manā bhava mad-bhakto
mad-yājī māṁ namaskuru...

"Engage your mind always in thinking of Me, offer obeisances, and worship Me. Being completely absorbed in Me, surely you will come to Me."

Kṛṣṇa says, You should always think of Me: let your mind always be engaged in Me, Kṛṣṇa. Just become My devotee. If you want to worship, just worship Me. If you want to offer respects, offer them to Me. And if you do this, then without a doubt you'll come to Me.

This is a very simple method. Always think of Kṛṣṇa. There is no loss, and the gain is very great.

So if one chants Hare Kṛṣṇa, one undergoes no material loss, but gains spiritually. So why not try it? There is no expenditure. Everything has some price, but the Hare Kṛṣṇa *mantra* is different. Lord Kṛṣṇa and His followers in disciplic succession do not sell it—rather, they distribute it freely. We simply say to everyone, "Chant Hare Kṛṣṇa. Dance in ecstasy." It is a very nice thing.

So, I have come to your country, England, and especially here to your home to explain this Kṛṣṇa consciousness movement. It is very beneficial. You are intelligent boys. So my request to you is that you try to understand this Kṛṣṇa consciousness philosophy with all your powers of reason and argument. Kṛṣṇa dāsa Kaviraja, the author of *Caitanya-caritāmṛta,* says, *śrī-kṛṣṇa-caitanya-dayā karaha vicāra, vicāra karile citte pābe camatkara:* "If you are indeed interested in logic and argument, kindly apply it to the mercy of Śrī Caitanya Mahāprabhu.* If you do so, you will find it to be strikingly wonderful." [Cc. Adi 8.15] So just apply your powers of judgment to the mercy of Lord Caitanya. If you scrutinize His mercy, you'll find it sublime.

We are not forcing people to accept the Kṛṣṇa consciousness movement. Rather, we are putting it before them for their judgment. Let them judge it. We are not a sectarian religious movement—Kṛṣṇa consciousness is a science. So we ask you to judge it scrutinizingly with all your intellect. And we are sure you will find it sublime. And if you find it sublime, then why not help put it before the world?

Have you read our book *Bhagavad-gītā As It Is?*

John Lennon: I've read bits of *Bhagavad-gītā.* I don't know which version it was. There are so many different translations.

Why Interpret Bhagavad-gītā?

Śrīla Prabhupāda: Yes, there are different translations, in which the authors have given their own interpretations of the text. Therefore I have prepared our *Bhagavad-gītā As It Is.* Even Indian authors sometimes misrepresent *Bhagavad-gītā.* For instance, Mahatma Gandhi was a great man, but he tried to give his own interpretation of the *Gītā.* Say you have a box for a fountain pen. Everyone knows it is a fountain pen box. But someone might say, "No, it is something else, that is my interpretation." Is that very good?

Interpretation is only required when things are not understood clearly. If everybody can understand that this box is a fountain pen box, where is the necessity for interpretation? *Bhagavad-gītā* is clear; it is just like sunlight, and sunlight

*Lord Caitanya, an incarnation of God who appeared five centuries ago in Bengal and taught that everyone should chant the holy name of Kṛṣṇa.

does not require the aid of a lamp.

Let me give you an example. The first verse of *Bhagavad-gītā* is:

dhṛtarāṣṭra uvāca
dharmakṣetre kurukṣetre
sāmavetā yuyutsavaḥ
mamakāḥ pāṇḍavāś caiva
kim akurvata sañjaya

Dhṛtarāṣṭra uvāca means that King Dhṛtarāṣṭra, the father of Duryodhana, is asking his secretary, Sañjaya, about his sons, who are facing the Pāṅḍavas on the battlefield of Kurukṣetra. *Māmakāḥ* means "my sons." *Pāṅḍavāḥ* refers to the sons of King Pāṅḍu, the younger brother of Dhṛtarāṣṭra. *Yuyutsavaḥ* means "with fighting spirit." So Dhṛtarāṣṭra is saying, "My sons and the sons of my younger brother Pāṅḍu are assembled on the battlefield "ready to fight each other." The place where the battle will be fought is called *kurukṣetra,* which is also *dharmakṣetra,* a place of pilgrimage. *Kim akurvata.* "Now that they have assembled at Kurukṣetra," asks Dhṛtarāṣṭra, "what will they do?" This place, Kurukṣetra, still exists in India. Have you been to India?

John Lennon: Yes. But not to that place. We went to Hṛṣīkeśa.

Śrīla Prabhupāda: Oh, Hṛṣīkeśa. Hṛṣīkeśa is also a famous place of pilgrimage. Similarly, Kurukṣetra is a place of pilgrimage, near Delhi. It has been known as a place of pilgrimage since the Vedic times. In the *Vedas* it is stated, *kurukṣetre dharmaṁ yājayet:* "If you want to perform a religious ceremony, you should go to Kurukṣetra." Therefore Kurukṣetra is called *dharmakṣetra,* or place of pilgrimage.

In other words, Kurukṣetra is an actual historical location. And the Pāṅḍavas and the sons of Dhṛtarāṣṭra are actual historical personalities. Their history is recorded in the *Mahābhārata.* But in spite of these facts, Gandhi interpreted *kurukṣetra* as "the body," and the Pāṅḍavas as "the senses." These things are going on, but we object. Why should anyone interpret *Bhagavad-gītā* like that when the facts are there, presented so clearly?

Half-baked Philosophies

Bhagavad-gītā is a very authoritative and popular book, so unscrupulous authors try to put forward their own half-baked philosophies in the guise of commentaries on the *Gītā*. Therefore, there are so many false and misleading interpretations of the *Gītā*—six hundred and sixty-four or so. Everyone thinks he can interpret the *Gītā* in his own way. But why? Why should this be allowed? We say no. No—you cannot interpret *Bhagavad-gītā*. Otherwise, what is the authority of *Bhagavad-gītā*? The author of *Bhagavad-gītā* did not leave it to be interpreted by third-class men. The author is Kṛṣṇa, the Supreme Lord. He said everything clearly. Why should an ordinary man interpret His words? That is our objection.

Therefore, we are presenting *Bhagavad-gītā* as it is. In *Bhagavad-gītā* you'll find very elevated philosophy and theology as well as sociology, politics, and science. Everything is there and everything is clearly explained by Kṛṣṇa. So this Kṛṣṇa consciousness movement means to present *Bhagavad-gītā* as it is. That's all. We have not manufactured anything.

[*A woman enters the room.*]

John Lennon: This is Dan's wife, Jill, who lives here with us, too.

Śrīla Prabhupāda: Oh, very glad to see you. Be happy and make all others happy. This is Kṛṣṇa consciousness. *Sarve sukhena bhavantu.* That is the Vedic idea: everyone be happy. Caitanya Mahāprabhu says the same thing. He wanted this Kṛṣṇa consciousness movement to be preached in every village and in every town of the world. It will make people happy. He foretold this. The purpose of any great mission, or of any high ideals, should be to make people happy, because in this material existence there is no happiness. That is a fact. There cannot be any happiness here.

Nature's Invincible Laws

This place is not meant for happiness. In *Bhagavad-gītā* Lord Kṛṣṇa Himself says that this world is *duhkhālayarm aśāśvatam. Duhkhālayam* means it is a place of miseries, and *aśāśvatam* means it is temporary. Everything here is temporary. So you might accept that this material world is a miserable place and say, "All right, it's miserable, but I accept it." But that attitude has no value, because the material nature will not even allow you to stay here and accept the misery. This world is *aśāśvatam,* temporary. You have to leave. But Kṛṣṇa says there is a way to end this miserable existence: "After attaining Me, the great souls, who are *yogīs* in devotion, never return to this temporary world, which is full of miseries, because they have attained the highest perfection." [Bg. 8.15] If somebody comes to Me, says Kṛṣṇa, then he doesn't have to return to the miserable conditions of life in the material world.

So, we should understand what Kṛṣṇa is saying here. Nature is so cruel. In America, President Kennedy thought he was the most fortunate man, the happiest man. He was young, he was elected President. He had nice wife and children and was respected all over the world. But within a second [Śrīla Prabhupāda snaps his finger] it was all finished. His position was temporary. Now, what is his condition? Where is he? If life is eternal, if the living entity is eternal, then where has he gone? What is he doing? Is he happy, or is he distressed? Has he been reborn in America or China? No one can say.

Changing Bodies

But it is a fact that, as a living entity, he's eternal, he's existing. That is the beginning of *Bhagavad-gītā's* philosophy. *Na hanyate hanyamāne śarīre*. After the destruction of this body, the living entity is not destroyed; he is still there. Just like in your childhood you had a small body. That body is no more, but you are still existing. So it is natural that when this body ceases to exist, you will continue to exist in another body. It's not very difficult to understand. The soul is eternal, and the body is temporary. That's a fact.

Therefore, this present life is meant for manufacturing the next body. That is Vedic knowledge. In this life we are creating our next body. For instance, a boy may be studying very nicely in school. In this way he is creating his adult body. As a young man he will enjoy the results of his boyhood education. By education he can get a nice job, a nice house. So in this sense we can say that the young boy at school is creating his next body. Similarly, we are all creating our next bodies according to our *karma*. By *karma,* most people will take another material body. But Kṛṣṇa says it is possible to create a spiritual body so that you can come to Him. He says that those who worship Him go to His spiritual planet after death. The whole Vedic philosophy teaches that if you want to go to a particular planet you must have a suitable body. You cannot go with this body. For instance, people are now trying to go to the moon planet. They are attempting to go with their material bodies, but they cannot stay there. But Kṛṣṇa gives the process for going to other planets, and the highest planet is Kṛṣṇa's planet. You can go there. "Those who worship the demigods will take birth among the demigods; those who worship ghosts and spirits will take birth among such beings; those who worship ancestors go to the ancestors; and those who worship Me will live with Me." [Bg. 9.25]

Such a person does not come back again to this miserable material condition. Why? He has attained the highest perfection, to go back to Kṛṣṇa. So this is the greatest benediction for human society, to train people to go back to Kṛṣṇa's spiritual planet, where they can dance with Kṛṣṇa in *rāsa-līlā*. Have you seen pictures of Kṛṣṇa's *rāsa-līlā* dancing?

John Lennon: Which picture?

Disciple: The paintings of Kṛṣṇa dancing with Rādhā and the cowherd girls, the *gopīs*.

John Lennon: Oh, you mean the one on the wall of the temple room?

Śrīla Prabhupāda: Yes. So, we can go to the spiritual world and join with Kṛṣṇa and dance happily, with no anxiety. Living beings can have so many different connections with Kṛṣṇa—as friend, as servant, as parents, as lover, whatever you like. Kṛṣṇa says, *ye yathā māṁ prapadyante tāṁs tathaiva bhajāmy aham:* "All of them—as they surrender unto Me—I reward accordingly." [Bg. 4.11] Just cultivate the consciousness of the particular relationship you desire with Kṛṣṇa. He is prepared to accept you in that capacity. And that makes a solution to all problems.

In this world, nothing is permanent, nothing is blissful, nothing is full of knowledge. So we are training Western boys and girls in the science of Kṛṣṇa consciousness. Anyone can take advantage of it. It is very beneficial. You should also try to understand it, and if you find it valuable, then please take it up. You are looking for something very nice. Is my proposal unreasonable? You are intelligent boys. Try to understand it.

Music and Mantras

And you also have very good musical abilities. The Vedic *mantras* were all transmitted through music. The *Sāma-veda,* in particular, is full of music:

yaṁ brahmā varuṇendra-rudra-marutaḥ
stunvanti divyaiḥ stavair
vedaiḥ sāṅga-pada-kramopaniṣadair
gāyanti yaṁ sāmagāḥ

"I offer my humble obeisances to the Supreme Lord, whom great demigods like Brahmā, Varuṇa, Indra, Śiva, and the Maruts praise with transcendental prayers. Those who know the *Sāma-veda* sing about Him with different Vedic hymns." [*Śrīmad-Bhagavatam* 12.13.1] *Sāmagāḥ* means the followers of the *Sāma-veda. Gāyanti* means that they are always engaged in music. Through musical vibrations they are approaching the Supreme. *Gāyanti* means singing. So, Vedic *mantras* are meant to be sung. *Bhagavad-gītā* and *Śrīmad-Bhāgavatam* can be sung, very nicely. This is the proper way of chanting Vedic *mantras.* Simply by hearing the vibration, people will receive benefit, even if they do not understand the meaning. [*Śrīla Prabhupāda then chants some* mantras *from* Śrīmad-Bhāgavatam.]

Simply by transcendental sound vibration everything can be achieved. What kind of philosophy are you following? May I ask?

John Lennon: Following?

Yoko Ono: We don't follow anything. We are just living

George Harrison: We've done meditation. Or I do my meditation—*mantra* meditation.

Śrīla Prabhupāda: Hare Kṛṣṇa is also *mantra.*

John Lennon: Ours is not a song, though.

George Harrison: No, no. It's chanting.

John Lennon: We heard it from Maharishi. A *mantra* each.

Śrīla Prabhupāda: His *mantras* are not public.

George Harrison: Not out loud... No.

John Lennon: No—it's a secret.

Śrīla Prabhupāda: There's a story about Rāmānujācārya a great Kṛṣṇa conscious spiritual master. His spiritual master gave him a *mantra* and said, "My dear boy, you chant this *mantra* silently. Nobody else can hear it. It is very secret." Rāmānujācārya asked his *guru,* "What is the effect of this *mantra*?" The *guru* said, "By chanting this *mantra* in meditation, you'll get liberation."

So Rāmānujācārya immediately went out to a big public meeting and said, "Everyone chant this *mantra.* You'll all be liberated." [*Laughter.*] Then he came back to his spiritual master, who was very angry, and said, "I told you that you should chant silently!" Rāmānujācārya said, "Yes, I have committed an offense. So whatever punishment you like you can give me. But because you told me that this *mantra* will give liberation, I have given it to the public. Let everyone be liberated, and let me go to hell—I am prepared. But if by chanting this *mantra* everyone can be liberated, let it be publicly distributed."

His spiritual master then embraced him, saying, "You are

greater than me."

You see? If a *mantra* has so much power, why should it be secret. It should be distributed. People are suffering. So Caitanya Mahāprabhu said to chant this Hare Kṛṣṇa *mantra* loudly. Anyone who hears it, even the birds and beasts, will become liberated.

Which Mantra to Chant

Yoko Ono: If Hare Kṛṣṇa is such a strong, powerful *mantra,* is there any reason to chant anything else? For instance, you talked about songs and different *mantras.* Is there any point in the chanting of another song or *mantra*?

Śrīla Prabhupāda: There are other *mantras,* but the Hare Kṛṣṇa *mantra* is especially recommended for this age. But other Vedic *mantras* are also chanted. As I told you, the sages would sit with musical instruments, like the *tamboura,* and chant them. For instance, Nārada Muni* is always chanting *mantras* and playing his stringed instrument, the *vīṇā.* So chanting out loud, with musical instruments, is not a new thing. It's been done since time immemorial. But the chanting of the Hare Kṛṣṇa *mantra* is especially recommended for this age. This is stated in many Vedic literatures, such as the *Brahmāṇḍa Purāṇa,* the *Kalisantaraṇa Upaniṣad,* the *Agni Purāṇa,* and so forth. And apart from the statements of the Vedic literature, Lord Kṛṣṇa Himself, in the form of Lord Caitanya, preached that everyone should chant the Hare Kṛṣṇa *mantra.* And many people followed Him. When a scientist discovers something, it becomes public property. People may take advantage of it. Similarly, if a *mantra* has potency, all people should be able to take advantage of it. Why should it remain secret? If a *mantra* is valuable, it is valuable for everybody. Why should it be for only a particular person?

John Lennon: If all *mantras* are just the name of God, then whether it's a secret *mantra* or an open *mantra* it's all the

---

*A liberated sage who travels throught the universe preaching love of God.

name of God. So it doesn't really make much difference, does it, which one you sing?

Śrīla Prabhupāda: It does make a difference. For instance, in a drug shop they sell all types of medicines for curing different diseases. But still you have to get a doctor's prescription in order to get a particular type of medicine. Otherwise, the druggist won't supply you. You might go to the drug shop and say, "I'm diseased. Please give me any medicine you have." But the druggist will ask you, "Where is your prescription."

Prescription for the Age of Kali

Similarly, in this age of Kali* the Hare Kṛṣṇa *mantra* is prescribed in the *śāstras*, or scriptures. And the great teacher Caitanya Mahāprabhu, whom we consider to be an incarnation of God, also prescribed it. Therefore, our principle is that everyone should follow the prescription of the great authorities. *Mahājano yena gataḥ sa panthāḥ*. We should follow in the footsteps of the great authorities. That is our business. The *Mahābhārata* states, "Dry arguments are inconclusive. A great personality whose opinion does not differ from others is not considered a great sage. Simply by study of the *Vedas*, which are variegated, one cannot come to the right path by which religious principles are understood. The solid truth of religious principles is hidden in the heart of an unadulterated self-realized person. Consequently, as the *śāstras* affirm, one should accept whatever progressive path the *mahājanas* advocate." [*Mahābhārata, Vana-parva*, 313.117] This Vedic *mantra* says that if you simply try to argue and approach the Absolute Truth, it is very difficult. By argument and reason it is very difficult, because our arguments and reason are limited. And our senses are imperfect. There are many confusing varieties of scriptures, and every philosopher has a different opinion, and unless a philosopher defeats other philosophers, he cannot become recognized as a big philosopher. One the-

---

*The present age, which began five thousand years ago, characterized in the ancient Vedic scriptures as the age of quarrel and hypocrisy.

ory replaces another, and therefore philosophical speculation will not help us arrive at the Absolute Truth. The Absolute Truth is very secret. So how can one achieve such a secret thing? You simply follow the great personalities who have already achieved success.

So our Kṛṣṇa consciousness philosophical method is to follow the great personalities, such as Lord Kṛṣṇa, Lord Caitanya, and the great spiritual masters in disciplic succession. Take shelter of bona fide authorities and follow them—that is recommended in the *Vedas*. That will take you to the ultimate goal.

In *Bhagavad-gītā* [4.1], Lord Kṛṣṇa also recommends this process: "The Blessed Lord said; I instructed this imperishable science of *yoga* to the sun-god, Vivasvān, and Vivasvān, instructed it to Manu, the father of mankind, and Manu in turn instructed it to Ikṣvāku." Kṛṣṇa is saying, My dear Arjuna, don't think that this science of Kṛṣṇa consciousness is something new. No. It is eternal, and I first spoke it to the sun-god, Vivasvān, and Vivasvān spoke it to his son Manu, and Manu also transferred this knowledge to his son, King Ikṣvāku.

The Lord further explains:

evaṁ paramparā-prāptam
imaṁ rajarṣayo viduḥ
sa kāleneha mahatā
yogo naṣṭaḥ parantapa

"This supreme science was thus received through the chain of disciplic succession, and the saintly kings understood it in that way. But in course of time, the succession was broken, and therefore the science as it is appears to be lost." [Bg. 4.2]

You Can't Manufacture a Mantra

Evaṁ paramparā-prāptam: In this way, by disciplic succession, the knowledge is coming down. *Sa kāleneha mahatā yogo naṣṭaḥ parantapa:* But in the course of time the succession was broken. Therefore, Kṛṣṇa says, I am speaking it to you again. So a *mantra* should be received from the disciplic succession. The Vedic injunction is *sampradāya-vihīnā ye mantrās te niṣphalā matāḥ*. If your *mantra* does not come through the disciplic succession, it will not be effective. *Mantrās te niṣphalāḥ. Niṣphalāḥ* means that it will not produce the desired result. So the *mantra* must be received through the proper channel, or it will not act. A *mantra* cannot be manufactured. It must come from the original Supreme Absolute, coming down through the channel of disciplic succession. It has to be received in that way, and only then will it act.

According to our Kṛṣṇa consciousness philosophy, the *mantra* is coming down through four channels of disciplic succession: one through Lord Śiva, one through the goddess Lakṣmī, one through Lord Brahmā, and one through the four Kumāras. The same thing comes down through different channels. These are called the four *sampradāyas,* or disciplic successions. So, one has to take his *mantra* from one of these four *sampradāyas;* then only is that *mantra* active. If we receive the *mantra* in that way, it will be effective. And if one does not receive his *mantra* through one of these *sampradāya* channels, then it will not act; it will not give fruit.

Yoko Ono: If the *mantra* itself has such power, does it matter where you receive it, where you take it?

Śrīla Prabhupāda: Yes, it does matter. For instance, milk is nutritious. That's a fact; everyone knows. But if milk is touched by the lips of a serpent, it is no longer nutritious. It becomes poisonous.

Yoko Ono: Well, milk is material.

Śrīla Prabhupāda: Yes, it is material. But since you are trying to understand spiritual topics through your material senses, we have to give material examples.

Yoko Ono: Well, no, I don't think you have to give me the material sense. I mean, the *mantra* is not material. It should be something spiritual; therefore, I don't think anybody should be able to spoil it. I wonder if anybody can actually

spoil something that isn't material.
Śrīla Prabhupāda: But if you don't receive the *mantra* through the proper channel, it may not really be spiritual.
John Lennon: How would you know, anyway? How are you able to tell? I mean, for any of your disciples or us or anybody else who goes to any spiritual master—how are we able to tell if he's for real or not?
Śrīla Prabhupāda: You shouldn't go to just any spiritual master.

Who's a Genuine Guru?

John Lennon: Yes, we should go to a true master. But how are we to tell one from the other?
Śrīla Prabhupāda: It is not that you can go to just any spiritual master. He must be a member of a recognized *sampradāya*, a particular line of disciplic succession.
John Lennon: But what if one of these masters who's not in the line says exactly the same thing as one who is? What if he says his *mantra* is coming from the *Vedas* and he seems to speak with as much authority as you? He could probably be right. It's confusing—like having too many fruits on a plate.
Śrīla Prabhupāda: If the *mantra* is actually coming through a bona fide disciplic succession, then it will have potency.
John Lennon: But the Hare Kṛṣṇa *mantra* is the best one?
Śrīla Prabhupāda: Yes.
Yoko Ono: Well, if Hare Kṛṣṇa is the best one, why should we bother to say anything else other than Hare Kṛṣṇa?
Śrīla Prabhupāda: It's true, you don't have to bother with anything else. We say that the Hare Kṛṣṇa *mantra* is sufficient for one's perfection, for liberation.
George Harrison: Isn't it like flowers Somebody may prefer roses, and somebody may like carnations better. Isn't it really a matter for the individual devotee to decide. One person may find that Hare Kṛṣṇa is more beneficial to his spiritual progress, and yet another person may find that some other *mantra* may be more beneficial for himself. Isn't it just a matter of

taste, like choosing a flower. They're all flowers, but some people may like one better than another.

Śrīla Prabhupāda: But still there is a distinction. A fragrant rose is considered better than a flower without any scent.

Yoko Ono: In that case, I can't...

Śrīla Prabhupāda: Let's try to understand this flower example.

Yoko Ono: O.K.

Śrīla Prabhupāda: You may be attracted by one flower, and I may be attracted by another flower. But among the flowers a distinction can be made. There are many flowers that have no fragrance and many that have fragrance.

Yoko Ono: Is that flower that has fragrance better?

Śrīla Prabhupāda: Yes. Therefore, your attraction for a particular flower is not the solution to the question of which is actually better. In the same way, personal attraction is not the solution to choosing the best spiritual process. In *Bhagavad-gītā* [4.11], Lord Kṛṣṇa says, "All of them—as they surrender unto Me—I reward accordingly. Everyone follows My path in all respects O son of Prtha." Kṛṣṇa is the Supreme Absolute. If someone wants to enjoy a particular relationship with Him, Kṛṣṇa presents Himself in that way. It's just like the flower example. You may want a yellow flower, and that flower may not have any fragrance. That flower is there; it's for you, that's all. But if someone wants a rose, Kṛṣṇa gives him a rose. You both get the flower of your choice, but when you make a comparative study of which is better, the rose will be considered better.

So Kṛṣṇa reveals Himself in different ways to different types of seekers. Realization of Kṛṣṇa, the Absolute Truth, is of three varieties: Brahman, Paramātmā, and Bhagavān. Brahman, Paramātmā, and Bhagavān are simply three different features of the Absolute Truth. The *jñānīs,* or empiric philosophers, reach the impersonal Brahman. The *yogīs* focus on the Supersoul, Paramātmā And the devotees aim at Bhagavān or Kṛṣṇa, the Supreme Personality of Godhead. But Kṛṣṇa and the Supersoul and the impersonal Brahman are not different. They are all like the light, which is opposed to darkness. But even in light there are varieties.

Three Features of the Absolute

In the *Vedas,* the three features of the Absolute truth are explained by the example of sunlight, sun globe, and sun-god. In the sunshine there is light, and in the sun globe there is also light. Within the sun globe dwells the predominating deity of the sun planet, and he must also be full of light. Otherwise, where does all the sun's light come from? Brahman, God's impersonal aspect, is compared to the sun's rays, Supersoul is like the sun globe, and Kṛṣṇa is like the personality of the sun-god. But taken together, they are all the sun. Nevertheless, the distinctions remain. For instance, just because the sunshine comes through the window to your room, you cannot say that the sun itself has come. That would be a mistake. The sun is many millions of miles away. In a sense, the sun is present in your room, but it is a question of degree. So the degrees of spiritual realization in Brahman, Paramātmā, and Bhagavān realization are different.

Yoko Ono: But you said that if the milk is touched by the lips of a serpent it will become poisonous. A lot of churches probably had good teachings in the beginning but over time their messages have deteriorated. Now how can a person decide if the message of Brahman that you're talking about will always remain in its pure state? How can you be sure it won't be poisoned by serpents?

Becoming Serious

Śrīla Prabhupāda: That's an individual matter. You have to become a serious student.

Yoko Ono: Well, what do you mean by "serious student"? I mean, we're born serious or born—you know—unserious.

Śrīla Prabhupāda: Being serious means that you understand the distinction between Brahman, Paramātmā, and Bhagavān.

Yoko Ono: But does it depend on knowledge? I mean, the

final judgement you make?

Śrīla Prabhupāda: Everything depends on knowledge. Without knowledge, how can we make progress. To be a serious student means to acquire knowledge.

Yoko Ono: But not always knowledgeable are the ones who...

Śrīla Prabhupāda: Yes, no one can know the Absolute Truth completely. That is because our knowledge is very imperfect. But still, as far as our knowledge allows, we should try to understand the Absolute Truth. The *Vedas* say, *avāṅ-mānasa-gocara.* The Absolute is so great and unlimited that it is not possible for us to know Him completely; our senses do not allow it. But we should try as far as possible. And it is possible, because, after all, we are part and parcel of the Absolute. Therefore, all of the qualities of the Absolute are there in us, but in minute quantity. But that minute quantity of the Absolute within us is very great when compared to material knowledge.

Liberated vs. Material Knowledge

Material knowledge is practically no knowledge whatsoever. It is covered knowledge. But when one is liberated, and attains liberated knowledge, his knowledge is very much greater than the greatest material knowledge. So, as far as possible, we should try to understand Brahman, Paramātmā, and Bhagavān. The *Śrīmad-Bhāgavatam* [1.2.11] states, "Learned transcendentalists who know the Absolute Truth call this nondual substance Brahman, Paramātmā, or Bhagavān." Now again what is the distinction among these three degrees of knowledge? Actually, knowledge of Brahman, knowledge of Paramātmā, and knowledge of Bhagavān are knowledge of the same thing.

There is another example in this connection. Imagine you are looking at a hill from a distant place. First of all you see a hazy form on the horizon like a cloud. Then if you proceed closer you'll see it as something green. And if you actually walk on the hill, you'll see so many varieties of life—animals, men, trees, and so forth. But from the distance you just see it vaguely like a cloud. So although the Absolute Truth is always the same, it appears differently from different angles of vision. From the Brahman point of view, it appears like a hill seen as a cloud. When viewed as Paramātmā, the Absolute can be compared to the vision of the hill as something green. And when the Absolute is realized as the Supreme Person, Bhagavān, it is just like seeing the hill from up close. You see everything in complete detail. So although the person who sees Brahman, the person who sees Paramātmā, and the person who sees Kṛṣṇa are all focusing on the same thing, their realization is different according to their respective positions. These things are very nicely explained in *Bhagavad-gītā* [10.8] wherein Lord Kṛṣṇa says, "I am the source of all spiritual and material worlds. Everything emanates from Me. The wise who know this perfectly engage in My devotional service and worship Me with all their hearts." Kṛṣṇa says, I am the source of everything—Brahman, Paramātmā, everything. Elsewhere in *Bhagavad-gītā* [14.27] it is clearly stated that Kṛṣṇa is the source of Brahman: *brahmaṇo hi pratiṣṭhāham*. So knowledge of Brahman and Paramātmā are included within knowledge of Kṛṣṇa. If one has knowledge of Kṛṣṇa, he automatically has knowledge of Paramātmā and Brahman. Such a person automatically achieves the result of the *yogic* principle of meditation, namely, realization of the Supersoul, Paramātmā. And he also achieves the result of empirical philosophical speculation, namely, realization of Brahman. Beyond that, he is situated personally in the service of the Supreme Lord, Kṛṣṇa. So if you make a comparative study, you'll find that knowledge of Kṛṣṇa includes all other knowledge. The *Vedas* confirm this: *yasmin vijñāte sarvam evam vijñātaṁ bhavati:* "If you understand the Supreme, then all knowledge becomes automatically revealed." And in *Bhagavad-gītā* it is stated, "Knowing this we have nothing more to know."

So, first of all we have to seriously study the Vedic knowledge. Therefore, I am asking you to become serious students.

By understanding Kṛṣṇa, you will understand everything. Paramātmā is the localized aspect of the Absolute Personality of Godhead. The Lord says, *īśvaraḥ sarva-bhūtānām hṛd-deśe 'rjuna tiṣṭhati:* "The Supreme Lord is situated in everyone's heart, O Arjuna." [Bg. 18.61] And Brahman is the effulgence of the Absolute. And Parambrahman, or Bhagavān, the Supreme Personality of Godhead, is Kṛṣṇa. So if you have full knowledge of Kṛṣṇa, then you also have knowledge of Brahman and knowledge of Paramātmā. But if you simply have knowledge of Brahman or knowledge of Paramātmā, you have no knowledge of Kṛṣṇa. Again we give the example of the sun. If you know the sunshine, you do not know the sun globe or the predominating deity in the sun. But if you are situated at the side of the sun-god, then you automatically possess knowledge of the sun globe and the sunshine.

Therefore, considered impartially, it is recommended that one should know the science of the Absolute Truth, or Kṛṣṇa. That will include all other knowledge. Kṛṣṇa says,

bahūnāṁ janmanām ante
jñānavān māṁ prapadyate
vāsudevaḥ sarvam iti
sa mahātmā sudurlabhaḥ

"After many births and deaths, he who is actually in knowledge surrenders unto Me, knowing Me to be the cause of all causes and all that is. Such a great soul is very rare." [Bg. 7.19] Kṛṣṇa says that after many, many births of cultivating knowledge, one actually becomes wise, *jñānavān. Jñānavān* means one who has attained wisdom. *Bahūnāṁ janmanām ante jñānavān māṁ prapadyate:* Such a wise man surrenders unto Me, Kṛṣṇa, Why? *Vāsudevaḥ sarvam iti:* He understands, Oh, Vāsudeva, Kṛṣṇa, is everything. *Sa mahātmā sudurlabhaḥ:* Such a great soul is very rare, Kṛṣṇa says, I am the origin; everything emanates from Me. One who knows this science perfectly is called *budha,* or intelligent, and he becomes engaged in Kṛṣṇa consciousness.

In *Vedānta-sūtra* the first aphorism is, *athāto brahma jijñāsā*. "Now is the time for inquiry about the Absolute, Brahman." So what is Brahman? The next aphorism is, *janmādy asya yataḥ*. Brahman, the Absolute, is that from whom everything is emanating." In *Bhagavad-gītā,* that Absolute Personality of Godhead Himself says, *mattaḥ sarvaṁ pravartate*—everything is emanating from Me. So if you study the Vedic literature very scrutinizingly, you will come to the conclusion that Kṛṣṇa is the Supreme. Therefore, Kṛṣṇa consciousness will include all other knowledge. If you have a million dollars, ten dollars is included, five hundred dollars is included, and a thousand dollars is also included. But one who only has ten dollars or five hundred dollars cannot claim that he has a million dollars. So, Kṛṣṇa consciousness includes all spiritual knowledge. That is accepted by all the *ācāryas,* or great spiritual masters.

Exploiting Bhagavad-gītā

You've been speaking of Maharishi. Hasn't he written some book on *Bhagavad-gītā*?

John Lennon: Yes, that's the one we've read.

Śrīla Prabhupāda: So, why is he using Kṛṣṇa's book to put forward his own philosophy? *Bhagavad-gītā* is Kṛṣṇa's book. Why is he taking Kṛṣṇa's book?

George Harrison: Well, he didn't. He just translated it.

Śrīla Prabhupāda: Why? Because Kṛṣṇa's book is very well respected.

John Lennon: I've also read part of another translation by Paramahansa Yogananda.

Śrīla Prabhupāda: Yes, all these men take advantage of Kṛṣṇa's book to lend an air of authority to their own speculations. Vivekananda has done it, Aurobindo has done it, Dr. Rādhākrishnan has done it, Mahatma Gandhi has done it. Thousands of them have done it. But why do they use *Bhagavad-gītā* as the vehicle for their ideas?

George Harrison: They just want to present it in English.

Śrīla Prabhupāda: No, no, it is not a question of English translation. It is a question of the thoughts in Kṛṣṇa's book. They are changing the thoughts. They may translate it into English or Persian; that doesn't matter. The big problem is that they are taking advantage of the authority of *Bhagavad-gītā* to put forward their own thoughts. Why should they quote from *Bhagavad-gītā* to prove their own thoughts, which are completely different from Kṛṣṇa's thoughts? If they are going to write about *Bhagavad-gītā,* they should leave out their own concocted thoughts and directly present the conclusions of the *Gītā.* Why not present the *Bhagavad-gītā* as it is? That is our proposition.

George Harrison: But *Bhagavad-gītā* as it is... It's in Sanskrit.

Śrīla Prabhupāda: No, we have translated it into English.

George Harrison: But they have also translated it into English.

John Lennon: Yes, they've translated it. You've translated it. They're all translations I mean...

Śrīla Prabhupāda: Yes, any *Bhagavad-gītā* that you read is a translation. You can't read the original,

George Harrison: Well which is the original?

Śrīla Prabhupāda: The original is there: the original is the Sanskrit.

Yoko Ono: Yes, it's in Sanskrit, but we don't read Sanskrit.

John Lennon: It's pointless me reading Sanskrit, because I don't understand the Sanskrit.

Śrīla Prabhupāda: Therefore you have to read a translation.

George Harrison: But there's a hundred translations.

John Lennon: And they all have different interpretations.

George Harrison: In all the versions I've read, the authors all claim that theirs is the best. And sometimes I get something from one which I didn't get from another.

Disciple: Did you ever read any without any commentary at all? Just straight?

George Harrison: Just the Sanskrit, you mean?

Disciple: No, just the translation.

His Divine Grace
A. C. Bhaktivedanta Swami Prabhupāda
Founder-Ācārya
of the Internatinal Society for Krishna Consciousness

In *Bhagavad-gītā*, Lord Kṛṣṇa explains how to achieve peace: "The sa
es, knowing Me as the ultimate purpose of all sacrifices and austeritie
the Supreme Lord of all planets and demigods, and the benefactor a
well-wisher of all living entities, attain peace from the pangs of materi
miseries." (*p. 1*)

137
HIGHGATE
vhf
95·3
BBC RADIO
news... travel... entertainment

PICCADILLY CIRCUS
STATION

Śrīla Prabhupāda with some of his disciples in the Temple Room at Joh
Lennon's Tittenhurst Park Estate.

A devotee chats with George Harrison in the grounds of the Tittenhurs
Park Estate in 1969.

n Lennon and Yoko Ono work and relax in the garden at their Titten-
rst Park Estate. 1969.

Śrīla Prabhupāda discusses philosophy with John Lennon, Yoko O
George Harrison and friends along with some of his disciples in his ro
at the Tittenhurst Park Estate.

hn Lennon and Yoko Ono take *prasādam* [food that has been offered to ṛṣṇa] with the devotees in the Temple Room at the Tittenhurst Estate.

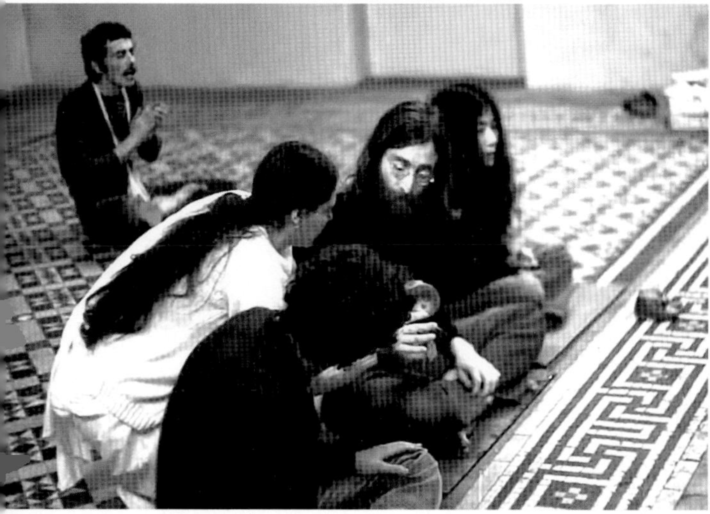

devotee shows John Lennon how to play *kartālas* in the Temple Room John's Tittenhurst Estate.

The London devotees perform *saṅkīrtana* on the occasion of Lord Ca
anya'a appearance day.

Śrīla Prabhupāda waits for his flight leaving London with some disciple

George Harrison: Well, that's really what they are. They all have a translation. Some of them have a commentary on top of that. But as far as the translations go, it just depends on who's translating as to what the translation is.

Who Has the Authority

Disciple: Right. So you have to go through the authorities.

John Lennon: But how do you know one authority from another?

George Harrison: The world is full of authorities, really, you know.

Yoko Ono: There's five hundred authorities, you know, who...

John Lennon: I found that the best thing for myself is to take a little bit from here and a little bit from there.

Yoko Ono: I mean, we're not just saying that. We want to ask your advice on that. In other words, what is your answer to this question of authority? You're saying that there are five hundred versions of *Bhagavad-gītā.* Now why would anyone translate the *Gītā* into English without authority? What is the authority, and who has the authority?

Śrīla Prabhupāda: The authority is the original text.

Yoko Ono: Yes, but everybody's translating from the original text.

Śrīla Prabhupāda: Yes.

Yoko Ono: So, what's the difference between one translation and another?

Disciplic Succession

Śrīla Prabhupāda: The whole question rests upon the principle of *sampradāya,* or disciplic succession. If we don't take the *Gītā* from the authorized disciplic succession, it won't help us. In our introduction to *Bhagavad-gītā* we have carefully explained that aside from Kṛṣṇa there is no authority. Kṛṣṇa is the authority, because *Bhagavad-gītā* was spoken by Kṛṣṇa. Can you deny that? Kṛṣṇa is the authority.

Yoko Ono: Yes, but did He translate the *Gītā* into English?

Śrīla Prabhupāda: The point is, Kṛṣṇa is the authority for *Bhagavad-gītā*. Do you accept this?
Yoko Ono: Yes.
Śrīla Prabhupāda: [*to John Lennon*]: is that all right?
John Lennon: Yes.
Śrīla Prabhupāda: Then you should see what Kṛṣṇa says. That is authoritative. Why should you hear a different opinion from someone else? So, if you want to understand what Kṛṣṇa has said, you have to search it out in the authorized Vedic literature. If you are a serious student, you will do it.
John Lennon: What about Yogananda, Maharishi, and all these other people who have translated the *Gītā*. How are we to tell that their version isn't also Kṛṣṇa's word?
Śrīla Prabhupāda: If you seriously want to understand this, you should study the original Sanskrit text.
John Lennon: Study Sanskrit? Oh, now you're talking.
George Harrison: But Vivekananda said that books and rituals and dogmas and temples are secondary details, anyway. He said they're not the most important thing. You don't have to read the book in order to have the perception.
Śrīla Prabhupāda: Then why did Vivekananda write so many books? [*Laughter.*]
George Harrison: Well, the same thing is said in the *Gītā*.
Śrīla Prabhupāda: No, the *Gītā* doesn't say that.
George Harrison: But in Hṛṣīkeśa, when we meditated for a long time, one man got tired of meditating, and he decided to read the *Gītā* so he could come out of meditation. He opened the *Gītā* and it said, "Don't read books. Meditate."
Śrīla Prabhupāda: Where does Kṛṣṇa say that in the *Gītā*?
George Harrison: The *Gītā* said it.

What Does Kṛṣṇa Say?

Śrīla Prabhupāda: No, in *Bhagavad-gītā* [13.5] Kṛṣṇa says,

ṛṣibhir bahudhā gītaṁ
chandobhir vividaiḥ pṛthak

brahma-sūtra-padaiś caiva
hetumadbhir viniścitaiḥ

"That knowledge of the field of activities and of the knower of activities is described by various sages in various Vedic writings—especially in the *Vedānta-sūtra*—and is presented with all reasoning as to cause and effect." He explains that the scientific knowledge of the Absolute Truth is explained very clearly in the *Brahma-sūtra,* or *Vedānta-sūtra.* The *Vedānta-sūtra* is a book. In another place in the *Gītā* [16.23], Kṛṣṇa says, "But he who discards scriptural injunctions and acts according to his own whims attains neither perfection nor happiness nor the supreme destination." These things are there in the *Gītā.* So how can you say that Kṛṣṇa has not recommended that we read books?

Yoko Ono: I see a pattern in what you've said. For instance, you said that Hare Kṛṣṇa is the most superpowerful word. And if that is true, then why do we bother to utter any other words? I mean, is it necessary And why do you encourage us, saying that we're songwriters and all, to write any other song than Hare Kṛṣṇa?

Śrīla Prabhupāda: Chanting the Hare Kṛṣṇa *mantra* is the recommended process for cleaning our hearts. So actually one who chants Hare Kṛṣṇa regularly doesn't have to do anything else. He is already in the correct position. He doesn't have to read any books.

Yoko Ono: Yes, I agree. So why do you say that it's all right to write songs, speak, and all that? It's a waste of time, isn't it?

Śrīla Prabhupāda: No, it's not a waste of time. For instance, Śrī Caitanya Mahāprabhu would spend most of His time simply chanting. He was a *sannyāsī,* a member of the renounced spiritual order of life. So, He was criticized by great *sannyāsīs,* who said, "You have become a *sannyāsī,* and yet You do not read the *Vedanta-sūtra.* You are simply chanting and dancing." In this way, they criticized His constant chanting of Hare Kṛṣṇa. But when Caitanya Mahāprabhu met such stalwart scholars, He did not remain silent. He established the chanting of Hare Kṛṣṇa by sound arguments based on the Vedic scriptures.

Chanting for Liberation

Chanting Hare Kṛṣṇa is sufficient for liberation; there is no doubt about it. But if someone wants to understand the Hare Kṛṣṇa *mantra* through philosophy, through study, through *Vedānta,* then we do not lack information. We have many books. But it is not that the Hare Kṛṣṇa *mantra* is somehow insufficient and therefore we are recommending books. The Hare Kṛṣṇa *mantra* is sufficient. But when Caitanya Mahāprabhu was chanting, He sometimes had to meet opposing scholars, such as Prakāśānanda Sarasvatī and Sārvabhauma Bhaṭṭācārya. And then He was ready to argue with them on the basis of *Vedānta.* So, we should not be dumb. If someone comes to argue with *Vedānta* philosophy, then we must be prepared. When we are preaching, many different types of people will come with questions. We should be able to answer them. Otherwise, the Hare Kṛṣṇa *mantra* is sufficient. It does not require any education, any reading, or anything else. Simply by chanting Hare Kṛṣṇa, you get the highest perfection. That's a fact.

Disciple: You were saying earlier today that we can also practice our Kṛṣṇa consciousness while we're working, hammering nails.

Śrīla Prabhupāda: Yes.

Disciple: So chanting along with devotional service, performing our duties while concentrating on Kṛṣṇa, is also part of the process, isn't it?

Śrīla Prabhupāda: Yes, the whole idea is *manaḥ kṛṣṇe niveśayet:* The mind should always be fixed on Kṛṣṇa, that is the process. You can do this through philosophy or through arguments or through chanting—any way you can. That is recommended in *Bhagavad-gītā* [6.47]: "And of all the *yogīs,* he who always abides in Me with great faith, worshipping Me in transcendental loving service is most intimately united with Me in *yoga* and is the highest of all." You might have read it. I think Maharishi has also translated this part of *Bhagavad-gītā*. Have you read it?

George Harrison: I haven't read all of his book. Just part of it

Śrīla Prabhupāda: So, this is the last verse of the Sixth Chapter of *Bhagavad-gītā*. You'll find it clearly stated there that of all *yogīs* the one whose mind is fixed up in Kṛṣṇa is the first-class *yogī*.

John Lennon: Whose is the little purple paperback *Gītā* that we all have?

Disciple: That's the one that Śrīla Prabhupāda wrote.

John Lennon: Oh, that's the one. I've got that in the office. There's another one by that guy, that Spanish guy.

Disciple: I think that one thing Śrīla Prabhupāda was explaining didn't quite get cleared up. That is, how do we discern which translation of the *Gītā* is most authoritative? He answered when he said that Kṛṣṇa is the authority; so we have to receive the *Gītā* in a channel from Kṛṣṇa. And there are only four lines of disciplic succession that come from Kṛṣṇa. And of these, only one is existing now, or two.

Guru's Guru's Guru's Guru

Yoko Ono: What do you mean by channel? Is it hereditary, or what?

Disciple: It means a line of disciplic succession. Śrīla Prabhupāda received the message from his spiritual master...

Śrīla Prabhupāda: It's just like a channel. You can understand very easily. For instance, you might send a money order to a friend. So, through which channel will he receive it? He'll receive it through the post office and not by any other channel. When the postman comes to deliver it, your friend is confident that the money has safely arrived. So we give some importance to the postman because he's the representative of the post office. Similarly, Kṛṣṇa is the original authority. And therefore Kṛṣṇa's representative is also an authority. And who is Kṛṣṇa's representative? He is the devotee of Kṛṣṇa. Therefore the devotee of Kṛṣṇa is an authority, at least on *Bhagavad-gītā*. So you have to receive *Bhagavad-gītā* from a devotee of Kṛṣṇa. If one does not know anything about Kṛṣṇa, how can he preach *Bhagavad-gītā*? This is common sense.

John Lennon: Who says who's actually in the line of descent? I mean, it's just like royalty...

Yoko Ono: That's what I was talking about.

John Lennon: I mean, Yogananda also claims to be in a line...

George Harrison: *Guru's guru's guru's guru...*

John Lennon: He talks about his *guru's guru's guru's guru,* like that. Maharishi claimed that all his *guru's guru's guru's guru's* went way back. I mean, how are we to know? I mean, it seems to be just a matter of deciding, you know.

Śrīla Prabhupāda: But Maharishi does not say anything about Kṛṣṇa.

George Harrison: His *guru* is Śaṅkarācārya.

John Lennon: But they all talk about God, and Kṛṣṇa's just a name for God, isn't it?

Śrīla Prabhupāda: Whatever Maharishi may be, his knowledge does not extend up to Kṛṣṇa, not up to His personal feature.

John Lennon: That's what he used to say in exactly the same way about anybody else.

Śrīla Prabhupāda: But factually he cannot be an authority, because he does not speak anything about Kṛṣṇa. If a postman comes and does not know anything about the post office, what kind of postman is he?

Yoko Ono: But he does talk about his post office.

Śrīla Prabhupāda: No, you cannot create your own post office. There is only one post office, the government post office.

Yoko Ono: Yes, of course—I'm sure there's only one post office.

Śrīla Prabhupāda: You cannot create your own post office. If a postman comes and says, "I belong to another post office," then at once you can know that he is unauthorized.

Yoko Ono: No, he says that his post office is the only post office, too.

Disciple: You've been to that post office, and you weren't satisfied with it. That's why you're here now. So you have to test.

What's Real?

John Lennon: That's what we're doing. We're going around. Actually, Yoko never met Maharishi. So, we're asking for advice about how to know what's real. I know people who have been wandering around for years, seeking *gurus* and seeking teachers. It's doing them all quite well. I mean, we can only judge on a material level by looking at your disciples and looking at other people's disciples and looking at ourselves, you know. And say here's thirty disciples—say seven of them look fairly spiritual, another ten look okay, and the others just look as though they're having trouble. We have to keep sifting through the sand to see who's got the best.

Śrīla Prabhupāda: Try to understand the principle of authority. You say that you want to know how to find out who's an authority. The answer to this question is that Kṛṣṇa is the real authority. There is no doubt about it. If it isn't true, then why does Maharishi comment on Kṛṣṇa's book? And why does Aurobindo comment on Kṛṣṇa's book? And why does Vivekanada comment on Kṛṣṇa's book? And why does Dr. Rādhākrishnan comment on Kṛṣṇa's book? That proves that Kṛṣṇa is the real authority. Even Śaṅkarācārya comments on Kṛṣṇa's book. Do you know Śaṅkarācārya's commentary on *Bhagavad-gītā*? In that commentary he accepts Kṛṣṇa as the Supreme Personality of Godhead: *Kṛṣṇas tu bhagavān svayam.* He accepts it. You say that Maharishi accepts Śaṅkarācārya, but Śaṅkarācārya accepts Kṛṣṇa as the Supreme Personality of Godhead.

George Harrison: Yes, but it's like the Bible...

Śrīla Prabhupāda: Now, don't go to the Bible. We're taking of Kṛṣṇa. [*Laughter.*] Just try to understand that Kṛṣṇa is the authority, He's accepted by everyone. You say that Maharishi belongs to Śaṅkarācārya's disciplic succession. But Śaṅkarācārya accepts Kṛṣṇa, not just as an authority, but as the Supreme Personality of Godhead. Śaṅkarācārya says this in his own commentary on the *Gītā:* "To Him, the Supreme God, Kṛṣṇa, be all salutations." So the real authority is one who has accepted Kṛṣṇa as the Supreme Lord.

Yoko Ono: Now, who said that?

Śrīla Prabhupāda: All the great spiritual authorities say it. Śaṅkarācārya says it. Rāmānujācārya says it. All the spiritual authorities in the bona fide disciplic successions say it. Śaṅkarācārya accepted that *Kṛṣṇas tu bhagavān svayam*— that Kṛṣṇa is the Supreme Personality of Godhead. And at the last stage of his life Śaṅkarācārya said:

bhaja govindaṁ bhaja govindaṁ
bhaja govindaṁ mūḍha-mate
samprāpte sannihite kāle
na hi na hi rakṣati dukṛñ-karaṇe

"You intellectual fools, just worship Govinda [Kṛṣṇa], just worship Govinda, just worship Govinda. Your grammatical knowledge and word jugglery will not save you at the time of death." He told his followers, "You rascal, fools! What are you dealing with. That will not save you. *Bhaja govindaṁ,* You should just worship Kṛṣṇa." *Mūḍha-mate* means "you rascal."

John Lennon: It means what?

Śrīla Prabhupāda: It means, "You rascal, just worship Kṛṣṇa and become a devotee of Kṛṣṇa. When death comes, all of this grammatical jugglery of words will not save you. Kṛṣṇa can save you. So *bhaja govindam.*" That is the instruction of Śaṅkarācārya.

Yoko Ono: But every sect says that—

Śrīla Prabhupāda: There is no question of any other sect. Kṛṣṇa is the center of every sect, if Kṛṣṇa is the center then there is no question of different sects. There is only the sect of Kṛṣṇa.

Kṛṣṇa Means God

John Lennon: Does Kṛṣṇa mean "God"?
Śrīla Prabhupāda: Yes, Kṛṣṇa means "God," and God means "Kṛṣṇa."
John Lennon: In the Bible or any other holy book, they all talk about one God. So it's just the one Being everywhere, in all the books. So why isn't Hare Kṛṣṇa or something similar in the Bible, then? I mean, that's the only other holy book I know, because I was brought up with the Bible.
Disciple: It is in the Bible. In Psalms it says, "Praise the Lord with every breath. Praise the Lord with drum and flute."
John Lennon: But they haven't got very good tunes. They haven't been passing on any good chants, have they? [*Laughter.*] I mean, would it be effective to chant, "Lord Jesus, Lord Jesus, hail Lord Jesus"?
Śrīla Prabhupāda: Lord Jesus says that he is the son of God. He's not God but the son of God. In that sense, there is no difference between Kṛṣṇa consciousness and Christianity. There is no quarrel between God and God's son. Jesus says to love God, and Kṛṣṇa, the Supreme Personality of Godhead, says, "Love Me." It's the same thing. If you say, "Love me," and your wife says, "Love my husband," there is no difference.
Yoko Ono: But about the knowledge—I'm a bit worried about it. So if you have to learn Sanskrit and all that, if that's the only way to get enlightenment, then what do you do about people who are not skillful in learning languages and things like that?
John Lennon: It's translated anyway.
Śrīla Prabhupāda: Yes, the translation is there.
John Lennon: You've got to take a risk.
Yoko Ono: But he said...
John Lennon: You've got to take the risk of reading a translated *Gītā.*
Śrīla Prabhupāda: Please try to understand one thing—that Kṛṣṇa is the authority. If Kṛṣṇa isn't the actual supreme authority, then why are all these people taking Kṛṣṇa's book and

translating it?

George Harrison: I'm not saying Kṛṣṇa isn't the Supreme. I believe that.

Śrīla Prabhupāda: Even if there are other sects, such as Maharishi's, they indirectly accept that Kṛṣṇa is the supreme authority. For instance, Maharishi belongs to the succession of Śaṅkarācārya, but we've seen that Sankarācārya accepts Kṛṣṇa as supreme.

George Harrison: We had a misunderstanding before about the translation of the Sanskrit *Gītā* into English. I was saying that there are many versions. And I think we thought you were trying to say that your version, your translation, was the only authoritative one and that the other translations were not. But we didn't really have any misunderstanding about the identity of Kṛṣṇa.

Śrīla Prabhupāda: That's all right. If you believe that Kṛṣṇa is the Supreme Lord, then you have to see who is addicted to Kṛṣṇa directly. One person may be chanting Kṛṣṇa's name twenty-four hours a day. And another person claiming to represent Kṛṣṇa says not a word about Kṛṣṇa; so how can he claim to be a devotee of Kṛṣṇa? How can he claim to be a representative of Kṛṣṇa. If Kṛṣṇa is the actual authority, then you should accept only those who are directly attached to Kṛṣṇa as His authorized representatives.

THE PEACE FORMULA

*...John and Yoko, Timmy Leary, Rosemary, Tommy Smothers, Bobby Dylan, Tommy Cooper, Derek Taylor, Norman Mailer, Alan Ginsberg, Hare Krishna, Hare Krishna. All we are saying is Give Peace a Chance.**

When John and Yoko recorded "Give Peace a Chance" in their room at Montreal's Queen Elizabeth Hotel, May 31, 1969, several Hare Kṛṣṇa devotees were there and sang along. They had visited with the Lennons for several days, discussing love, peace, and self-realization. John told Vibhavati dasi, "We want Kṛṣṇa consciousness, we want peace, the same formula your spiritual master tells about."

Written during the antiwar protests of late 1966, and published as a leaflet, Śrīla Prabhupāda's "Peace Formula—An entirely new approach to the antiwar question," profoundly affected the lives of thousands of Americans.

The great mistake of modern civilization is to encroach upon others' property as though it were one's own and thereby create an unnecessary disturbance of the laws of nature. These laws are very strong. No living entity can violate them. Only one who is Kṛṣṇa conscious can easily overcome the stringent laws of nature and thus become happy and peaceful in the world.

As a state is protected by the department of law and order, so the state of the universe, of which this earth is only an insignificant fragment, is protected by the laws of nature. This material nature is one of the different potencies of God, who is the ultimate proprietor of everything that be. This earth is, therefore, the property of God, but we, the living entities, especially the so-called civilized human beings, are

*"Give Peace A Chance," ©1969 Northern Songs, Limited

claiming God's property as our own under both an individual and collective false conception. If you want peace, you have to remove this false conception from your mind and from the world. This false claim of proprietorship by the human race on earth is partly or wholly the cause of all disturbances of peace on earth.

Foolish so-called civilized men are claiming proprietary rights on the property of God because they have now become godless. You cannot be happy and peaceful in a godless society. In the *Bhagavad-gītā* Lord Kṛṣṇa says that He is the factual enjoyer of all activities of the living entities, that He is the Supreme Lord of all universes, and that He is the well-wishing friend of all beings. When the people of the world know this as the formula for peace, it is then and there that peace will prevail.

Therefore, if you want peace at all, you will have to change your consciousness into Kṛṣṇa consciousness, both individually and collectively, by the simple process of chanting the holy name of God. This is the standard and recognized process for achieving peace in the world. We therefore recommend that everyone become Kṛṣṇa conscious by chanting Hare Kṛṣṇa, Hare Kṛṣṇa, Kṛṣṇa Kṛṣṇa, Hare Hare. Hare Rama, Hare Rama, Rama Rama, Hare Hare.

This is practical, simple, and sublime. Five hundred years ago this formula was introduced in India by Lord Śrī Caitanya, and now it is available throughout the world. Take to this simple process of chanting as above mentioned, realize your factual position by reading the *Bhagavad-gītā As It Is,* and reestablish your lost relationship with Kṛṣṇa, God. Peace and prosperity will be the immediate worldwide result.

CHANTING THE HARE KṚṢṆA MANTRA

The following exchange between John Lennon, Yoko Ono, and freelance writer Eve Norton appeared in the Montreal Star *in June 1969.*

Reporter: Where do you get your strength?
John Lennon: From Hare Kṛṣṇa.
Yoko: That's where we get it from, you know. We're not denying it.
John: We don't mind arguing with a few disciples, but Hare Kṛṣṇa's where it's at. And whether we get round to chanting, only time will tell. It's not where we are at right now, but we fully believe in it.

Brought to the West fifteen years ago by Śrīla Prabhupāda, "Hare Kṛṣṇa" has now become a household word. But what does it mean? In this short essay from the LP Kṛṣṇa Consciousness, *which introduced John Lennon and George Harrison to the chanting, Śrīla Prabhupāda explains the meaning of the Hare Kṛṣṇa* mantra.

The transcendental vibration established by the chanting of Hare Kṛṣṇa, Hare Kṛṣṇa, Kṛṣṇa Kṛṣṇa, Hare Hare/ Hare Rama, Hare Rama, Rama Rama, Hare Hare, is the sublime method for reviving our transcendental consciousness

As living spiritual souls, we are all originally Kṛṣṇa conscious entities, but due to our association with matter from time immemorial, our consciousness is now adulterated by the material atmosphere. The material atmosphere, in which we are now living, is called *māyā,* or illusion. *Māyā* means that which is not. And what is this illusion? The illusion is that we are all trying to be lords of material nature, while actually we are under the grip of her stringent laws. When a servant artificially tries to imitate the all-powerful master, it is called illusion. We are trying to exploit the resources of material nature, but actually we are becoming more and more entangled in her complexities. Therefore, although we are engaged in a hard struggle to conquer nature, we are ever more dependent on her. This illusory struggle against material nature can be stopped at once by revival of our eternal Kṛṣṇa consciousness.

Hare Kṛṣṇa, Hare Kṛṣṇa, Kṛṣṇa Kṛṣṇa, Hare Hare is the transcendental process for reviving this original pure consciousness. By chanting this transcendental vibration, we can cleanse away all misgivings within our hearts. The basic principle of all such misgivings is the false consciousness that I am the lord of all I survey.

Kṛṣṇa consciousness is not an artificial imposition on the mind. This consciousness is the original natural energy of the living entity. When we hear the transcendental vibration, this consciousness is revived. This simplest method of meditation is recommended for this age. By practical experience also, one can perceive that by chanting this *mahā-mantra,* or the Great Chanting for Deliverance, one can at once feel a transcendental ecstasy coming through from the spiritual stratum.

In the material concept of life we are busy in the matter of sense gratification as if we were in the lower animal stage. A little elevated from this status of sense gratification, one is engaged in mental speculation for the purpose of getting out of the material clutches. A little elevated from this speculative status, when one is intelligent enough, one tries to find out the supreme cause of all causes—within and without. And when one is factually on the plane of spiritual understanding, surpassing the stages of sense, mind and intelligence, he is then on the transcendental plane. This chanting of the Hare Kṛṣṇa *mantra* is enacted from the spiritual platform, and thus this sound vibration surpasses all lower strata of consciousness—namely sensual, mental and intellectual. There is no need, therefore, to understand the language of the *mantra,* nor is there any need for mental speculation nor any intellectual adjustment for chanting this *mahā-mantra*. It is automatic, from the spiritual platform, and as such, anyone can take part in vibrating this transcendental sound without any previous qualification. In a more advanced stage, of course, one is not expected to commit offenses on grounds of spiritual understanding.

In the beginning, there may not be the presence of all transcendental ecstasies, which are eight in number. These are: (1) Being stopped as though dumb, (2) perspiration, (3) standing up of hairs on the body, (4) dislocation of voice, (5) trembling, (6) fading of the body, (7) crying in ecstasy, and (8) trance. But there is no doubt that chanting for a while takes one immediately to the spiritual platform, and one shows the first symptom of this in the urge to dance along with the chanting of the *mantra*. We have seen this practically. Even a child can take part in the chanting and dancing. Of course, for one who is too entangled in material life, it takes a little more time to come to the standard point, but even such a materially engrossed man is raised to the spiritual platform very quickly. When it is chanted by a pure devotee of the Lord in love, it has the greatest efficacy on hearers, and as such this chanting should be heard from the lips of a pure devotee of the Lord, so that immediate effects can be achieved. As far as possible, chanting from the lips of nondevotees should be avoided. Milk touched by the lips of a serpent has poisonous effects.

The word Hari is the form of addressing the energy of the Lord, and the words Kṛṣṇa and Rāma are forms of addressing the Lord Himself. Both Kṛṣṇa and Rāma mean the supreme pleasure, and Hari is the supreme pleasure energy of the Lord, changed to Hare (Hah-ray) in the vocative. The supreme pleasure energy of the Lord helps us to reach the Lord.

The material energy, called *māyā,* is also one of the multi-energies of the Lord. And we the living entities are also the energy, marginal energy, of the Lord. The living entities are described as superior to material energy. When the superior energy is in contact with the inferior energy, an incompatible situation arises; but when the superior marginal energy is in contact with the superior energy, called Hari, it is established in its happy, normal condition.

These three words, namely Hari, Kṛṣṇa and Rāma, are the transcendental seeds of the *mahā-mantra*. The chanting is a spiritual call for the Lord and His energy, to give protection to the conditioned soul. This chanting is exactly like the genuine cry of a child for its mother's presence. Mother Hari helps the devotee achieve the Lord Father's grace, and the Lord reveals Himself to the devotee who chants this *mantra* sincerely.

No other means of spiritual realization is as effective in this age of quarrel and hypocrisy as the *mahā-mantra:* Hare Kṛṣṇa, Hare Kṛṣṇa, Kṛṣṇa Kṛṣṇa, Hare Hare/ Hare Rama, Hare Rama, Rama Rama, Hare Hare.

JOHN LENNON'S PAST LIFE REVEALED

Tridandi Goswami

A.C. Bhaktivedanta Swami

Founder-Acharya:
International Society for Krishna Consciousness

CENTER Los Angeles DATE 24 April 1970

My Dear Shyamsundar,

Please accept my blessings. I am in due receipt of your letter dated 20th April,1970 and have noted the contents carefully. You have asked me to disclose my dream about John Lennon.

I dreamt that John was showing me a house in Calcutta, a big palatial building, which formaly belonged to a very rich man, who was also a famous musician. The fact is that John Lennon was previously that wealthy Indian musician and now he has taken birth in England.

He has inherited his past musical talent, and because in his previous life he was very liberal and charitable he has now become very wealthy. Now in this life, if he utalizes his talents for giving the world Krishna Consciousness, he will achieve the highest perfection of life.

I hope this meets you in good health.

Your ever well-wisher.

A.C. Bhaktivedanta Swami

ACBS: db

Sriman Shyamasundar Das Adhikary
C/o George Harrison
Friar Park
Oxfordshire, England

*Editor's Note: The letter printed above was written by Śrīla Prabhupāda to one of his disciples on April 24, 1970. The Ve-*das *confirm that a spiritual master who is a pure devotee of Kṛṣṇa is empowered by the Lord with the mystic perfection of* tri-kāla jna, *the ability to know the past, present, and future lives of every human being.*

REINCARNATION AND BEYOND

> *"Why in the world are we here? Surely not to live in pain and fear.... Well, we all shine on, like the moon and the stars and the sun. Yeh, we all shine on."**

Have we been here before? Will we return again? What happens to the soul at death? How does reincarnation work? In this 1976 interview with Mike Robinson of the London Broadcasting Company, Śrīla Prabhupāda explains that reincarnation is not a matter of belief or faith, but a scientific, immutable law of the universe.

Mike Robinson: Can you tell me what you believe—what the philosophy of the Hare Kṛṣṇa movement is?
Śrīla Prabhupāda: Yes. Kṛṣṇa consciousness is not a question of belief; it is a science. The first step is to know the difference between a living body and a dead body. What is the difference? The difference is that when someone dies, the spirit soul, or the living force, leaves the body. And therefore the body is called "dead." So, there are two things: one, this body; and the other, the living force within the body. We speak of the living force within the body. That is the difference between the science of Kṛṣṇa consciousness, which is spiritual, and ordinary material science. As such, in the beginning it is very, very difficult for an ordinary man to appreciate our movement. One must first understand that he is a soul, or something other than his body.
Mike Robinson: And when will we understand that?
Śrīla Prabhupāda: You can understand at any moment, but it requires a little intelligence. For example, as a child grows, he becomes a boy, the boy becomes a young man, the young man becomes an adult, and the adult becomes an old man. Throughout all this time, although his body is changing from

*"Instant Karma," ©1969 Northern Songs, Limited

a child to an old man, he still feels himself to be the same person, with the same identity. Just see: the body is changing, but the occupier of the body, the soul, is remaining the same. So we should logically conclude that when our present body dies, we get another body. This is called transmigration of the soul.

Mike Robinson: So when people die it is just the physical body that dies?

Śrīla Prabhupāda: Yes. That is explained very elaborately in the *Bhagavad-gītā* (2.20): *na jāyate mriyate vā kadācin... na hanyate hanyamāne śarīre.*

Mike Robinson: Do you often quote references?

Śrīla Prabhupāda: Yes, we quote many references. Kṛṣṇa consciousness is a serious education, not an ordinary religion. [*To a devotee*] Find that verse in the *Bhagavad-gītā.*

Disciple:

na jāyate mriyate vā kadācin
nāyaṁ bhūtvā bhavitā vā na bhūyaḥ
ajo nityaḥ śāśvato 'yaṁ purāṇo
na hanyate hanyamāne śarīre

"For the soul, there is never birth nor death. Nor, having once been, does he ever cease to be. He is unborn, eternal, ever-existing, undying, and primeval. He is not slain when the body is slain."

Mike Robinson: Thank you very much for reading that. So can you explain to me just a bit more? If the soul is undying, does everybody's soul go to be with God when they die?

Śrīla Prabhupāda: Not necessarily. If one is qualified—if he qualifies himself in this life to go back home, back to Godhead—then he can go. If he does not qualify himself, then he gets another material body. And there are 8,400,000 different bodily forms. According to his desires and *karma,* the laws of nature give him a suitable body. It is just like when a man contracts some disease and then develops that disease. Is that difficult to understand?

Mike Robinson: It's very difficult to understand all of it.
Śrīla Prabhupāda: Suppose somebody has contracted smallpox. So, after seven days he develops the symptoms. What is that period called?
Mike Robinson: Incubation?

You're Not Free

Śrīla Prabhupāda: Incubation. So you cannot avoid it. If you have contracted some disease it will develop, by nature's law. Similarly, during this life you associate with various modes of material nature, and that association will decide what kind of body you are going to get in the next life. That is strictly under the laws of nature. Everyone is controlled by the laws of nature—they're completely dependent—but out of ignorance people think that they are free. They're not free; they're imagining that they're free, but they are completely under the laws of nature. So, your next birth will be decided according to your activities—sinful or pious, as the case may be.
Mike Robinson: Your Grace, could you go back over that just for a minute? You said that nobody is free. Are you saying that if we live a good life, we in some way determine a good future for ourselves?
Śrīla Prabhupāda: Yes.
Mike Robinson: So we are free to choose what we believe to be important? Religion is important, because if we believe in God and lead a good life...
Śrīla Prabhupāda: It is not a question of belief. Do not bring in this question of belief. It is law. For instance, there is a government. You may believe or not believe, but if you break the law, you'll be punished by the government. Similarly, whether you believe or don't believe, there is a God. If you don't believe in God and you independently do whatever you like, then you'll be punished by the laws of nature.
Mike Robinson: I see. Does it matter what religion you believe? Would it matter if one was a devotee of Kṛṣṇa?
Śrīla Prabhupāda: It is not a question of religion. It is a ques-

tion of science. You are a spiritual being, but because you are materially conditioned, you are under the laws of material nature. So you may believe in the Christian religion, and I may believe in the Hindu religion, but that does not mean that you are going to become an old man and I am not. We're talking of the science of growing old. This is natural law. It is not that because you are Christian you are becoming old or because I am Hindu I am not becoming old. Everyone is becoming old. So, similarly, all the laws of nature are applicable to everyone. Whether you believe this religion or that religion, it doesn't matter.

Mike Robinson: So, you're saying that there's only one God controlling all of us?

Śrīla Prabhupāda: There's one God, and one nature's law, and we are all under that nature's law. We are controlled by the Supreme. So if we think that we are free or that we can do anything we like, that is our foolishness.

Mike Robinson: I see. Can you explain to me what difference it makes, being a member of the Hare Kṛṣṇa movement?

Śrīla Prabhupāda: The Hare Kṛṣṇa movement is meant for those who are serious about understanding this science. There's no question of our being some sectarian group. No. Anyone can join. Students in college can be admitted. You may be a Christian, you may be a Hindu, you may be a Muhammadan—it doesn't matter. The Kṛṣṇa consciousness movement admits anyone who wants to understand the science of God.

You're a Soul

Mike Robinson: And what difference would it make to someone—being taught how to be a Hare Kṛṣṇa person?

Śrīla Prabhupāda: His real education would begin. The first thing is to understand that you are a spirit soul. And because you are a spirit soul, you are changing your body. This is the ABC of spiritual understanding. So, when your body is finished, annihilated, you are not finished. You get another body, just as you may change your coat and shirt. If you come to see me tomorrow wearing a different shirt and a different coat, does that mean you are a different person? No. Similarly, each time you die you change bodies, but you, the spirit soul within the body, remain the same. This point has to be understood; then one can make further progress in the science of Kṛṣṇa consciousness.

Mike Robinson: I am beginning to understand, but what I'm finding difficult is how this ties in with the large numbers of your people we see handing out Hare Kṛṣṇa literature on Oxford Street.

Śrīla Prabhupāda: This literature is meant to convince people about the need for spiritual life.

Mike Robinson: And you're really not concerned whether or not they join the Hare Kṛṣṇa movement?

Śrīla Prabhupāda: It doesn't matter. Our mission is to educate them. People are in ignorance; they are living in a fool's paradise, thinking that when their body is finished, everything is finished. That is foolishness.

Mike Robinson: And you are basically just concerned to tell them that there is a spiritual dimension to life?

Śrīla Prabhupāda: Our first concern is to tell you that you are not this body, that the body is your covering (your shirt and coat) and that within the body you are living.

Transmigration of the Soul

Mike Robinson: Yes, I think I've got that now. If we could go on from there—you said that how you lived made a difference in your life after death, that there are natural laws that determine your next life. How does the process of transmigration work?

Śrīla Prabhupāda: The process is very subtle. The spirit soul is invisible to our material eyes. It is atomic in size. After the destruction of the gross body, which is made up of the senses, blood, bone, fat, and so forth, the subtle body of mind, intelligence, and ego goes on working. So at the time of death this subtle body carries the small spirit soul to another gross body. The process is just like air carrying a fragrance. Nobody can see where this rose fragrance is coming from, but we know that it is being carried by the air. You cannot see how, but it is being done. Similarly, the process of transmigration of the soul is very subtle. According to the condition of the mind at the time of death, the minute spirit soul enters into the womb of a particular mother through the semen of a father, and then the soul develops a particular type of body given by the mother. It may be a human being, it may be a cat, a dog, or anything.

Mike Robinson: Are you saying that we were something else before this life?

Śrīla Prabhupāda: Yes.

Mike Robinson: And we keep coming back as something else the next time?

Śrīla Prabhupāda: Yes, because you are eternal. According to your work, you are simply changing bodies. Therefore, you should want to know how to stop this business, how you can remain in your original, spiritual body. That is Kṛṣṇa consciousness.

Mike Robinson: I see. So if I become Kṛṣṇa conscious, I wouldn't risk coming back as a dog?

Śrīla Prabhupāda: No. [*To a devotee*] Find this verse: *janma karma ca me divyam...*

Disciple:

janma karma ca me divyam
evaṁ yo vetti tattvataḥ
tyaktvā dehaṁ punar janma
naiti mām eti so 'rjuna

"One who knows the transcendental nature of My appearance and activities does not, upon leaving the body, take his birth again in this material world, but attains My eternal abode, O Arjuna." (Bg. 4.9)

Śrīla Prabhupāda: God is saying, "Anyone who understands

Me is free from birth and death." But one cannot understand God by materialistic speculation. That is not possible. One must first come to the spiritual platform. Then he gets the intelligence required to understand God. And when he understands God, he does not get any more material bodies. He goes back home, back to Godhead. He lives eternally; no more change of body.

Mike Robinson: I see. Now, you've read twice from your scriptures. Where do these scriptures come from? Can you briefly explain that?

Śrīla Prabhupāda: Our scriptures are coming from Vedic literature, which has existed from the beginning of creation. Whenever there is some new material creation—like this microphone, for instance—there is also some literature explaining how to deal with it. Isn't that so?

Mike Robinson: Yes, that's right, there is.

Śrīla Prabhupāda: And that literature comes along with the creation of the microphone.

Mike Robinson: That's right, yes.

Śrīla Prabhupāda: So, similarly, the Vedic literature comes along with the cosmic creation, to explain how to deal with it.

Mike Robinson: I see. So, these scriptures have been in existence since the beginning of creation. Now, if we could move on to something I believe you feel very strongly about. What is the main difference between Kṛṣṇa consciousness and the other Eastern disciplines being taught in the West?

Śrīla Prabhupāda: The difference is that we are following the original literature, and they are manufacturing their own literature. That is the difference. When there is some question on spiritual matters, you must consult the original literature, not some literature issued by a bogus man.

Mike Robinson: What about the chanting of Hare Kṛṣṇa, Hare Kṛṣṇa...

Śrīla Prabhupāda: Chanting Hare Kṛṣṇa is the easiest process by which to become purified, especially in this age, when people are so dull that they cannot very easily understand spiritual knowledge. If one chants Hare Kṛṣṇa, then his intelligence becomes purified, and he can understand spiritual things.

Mike Robinson: Can you tell me how you are guided in what you do?

Śrīla Prabhupāda: We take guidance from the Vedic literature.

Mike Robinson: From the scriptures you quoted?

Śrīla Prabhupāda: Yes, it's all in the literatures. We're explaining them in English. But we're not manufacturing anything. If we were to manufacture knowledge, then everything would be spoiled. The Vedic literature is something like the literature that explains how to set up this microphone. It says, "Do it like this: some of the screws should be on this side, around the metal." You cannot make any change; then everything would be spoiled. Similarly, because we are not manufacturing anything, one simply has to read one of our books, and he receives real spiritual knowledge.

You're Not this Body

Mike Robinson: How can the philosophy of Kṛṣṇa consciousness affect the way people live?

Śrīla Prabhupāda: It can relieve people's suffering. People are suffering because they are misunderstanding themselves to be the body. If you think that you are your coat and shirt, and you very carefully wash the coat and shirt but you forget to eat, will you be happy?

Mike Robinson: No, I wouldn't.

Śrīla Prabhupāda: Similarly, everyone is simply washing the "coat and shirt" of the body, but forgetting about the soul within the body. They have no information about what is within the "coat and shirt" of the body. Ask anybody what he is, and he will say, "Yes, I am an Englishman," or "I am an Indian." And if we say, "I can see you have an English or an Indian body, but what are you?"—That he cannot say.

Mike Robinson: I see.

Śrīla Prabhupāda: The whole modern civilization is operating on the misunderstanding that the body is the self (*dehātma-buddhi*). This is the mentality of the cats and dogs. Suppose I try to enter England, and you stop me at the border: "I am an Englishman," you say, "but you are Indian. Why have you come here?" And the dog barks, "*Rau, rau,* why are you coming?" So what is the difference in mentality? The dog is thinking he's a dog and I'm a stranger, and you are thinking you are an Englishman and I am an Indian. There's no difference in mentality. So if you keep people in the darkness of a dog's mentality and declare that you are advancing in civilization, you are most misguided.

Stopping Death

Mike Robinson: Now, moving on to another point, I gather the Hare Kṛṣṇa movement has some concern for areas of the world where there is suffering.
Śrīla Prabhupāda: Yes, we have the only concern. Others are simply avoiding the main problems: birth, old age, disease, and death. Others have no solutions to these problems; they are simply talking all kinds of nonsense. People are being misguided. They are being kept in darkness. Let us start to give them some light.
Mike Robinson: Yes, but apart from giving spiritual enlightenment, are you also concerned for people's physical well-being?
Śrīla Prabhupāda: Physical well-being automatically follows spiritual well-being.
Mike Robinson: And how does that work?
Śrīla Prabhupāda: Suppose you have a car. So, naturally, you take care of the car as well as yourself. But you don't identify yourself as the car. You don't say, "I am this car." That is nonsense. But this is what people are doing. They are taking too much care of the bodily "car," thinking that the car is the self. They forget that they are different from the car, that they are a spirit soul and have a different business. Just as no one

can drink petrol and be satisfied, no one can be satisfied with bodily activities. One must find out the proper food for the soul. If a man thinks, "I am a car, and I must drink this petrol," he is considered insane. Similarly, one who thinks that he is this body, and who tries to become happy with bodily pleasures, is also insane.

Do Animals Have Souls

Mike Robinson: There's a quote here that I'd like you to comment on. I was given this literature by your people before I came, and one of the things you say here is that "Religion without a rational basis is just sentiment." Can you explain that?

Śrīla Prabhupāda: Most religious people say, "We believe..." But what is the value of this belief? You may believe something which is not actually correct. For instance, some of the Christian people say, "We believe that animals have no soul." That is not correct. They believe animals have no soul because they want to eat the animals, but actually animals do have a soul.

Mike Robinson: How do you know that the animal has a soul?

Śrīla Prabhupāda: You can know, also. Here is the scientific proof: the animal eats, you eat; the animal sleeps, you sleep; the animal has sex, you have sex; the animal also defends, you also defend. Then what is the difference between you and the animal? How can you say that you have a soul but the animal doesn't?

Mike Robinson: I can see that completely. But the Christian scriptures say...

Śrīla Prabhupāda: Don't bring in any scriptures; this is a common sense topic. Try to understand. The animal is eating, you are eating; the animal is sleeping, you are sleeping; the animal is defending, you are defending; the animal is having sex, you are having sex; the animals have children, you have children; they have a living place, you have a living place. If the animal's body is cut, there is blood; if your body is cut, there is blood. So, all these similarities are there. Now, why do you deny this one similarity, the presence of the soul? This is not logical. You have studied logic? In logic there is something called analogy. Analogy means drawing a conclusion by finding many points of similarity. If there are so many points of similarity between human beings and animals, why deny one similarity? That is not logic. That is not science.

Mike Robinson: But if you take that argument and use it the other way...

Śrīla Prabhupāda: There is no other way. If you are not arguing on the basis of logic, then you are not rational.

Mike Robinson: Yes, OK, but let's start from another hypothesis. Suppose we assume that a human being has no soul...

Brainless Scientists

Śrīla Prabhupāda: Then you must explain the difference between a living body and a dead body. I have already explained this at the beginning. As soon as the living force, the soul, is gone from the body, even the most beautiful body has no value. No one cares for it; it's thrown away. But now, if I touch your hair, there will be a fight. That is the distinction between a living body and a dead body. In a living body the soul is there, and in a dead body the soul is not there. As soon as the soul leaves the body, the body has no value. It is useless. This is very simple to understand, but even the biggest so-called scientists and philosophers are too dull-headed to understand it. Modern society is in a very abominable condition. There is no man with a real brain.

Mike Robinson: Are you referring to all the scientists who fail to understand the spiritual dimension in life?

Śrīla Prabhupāda: Yes. Real science means full knowledge of everything, material and spiritual.

Mike Robinson: But you were a chemist in secular life, were you not?

Śrīla Prabhupāda: Yes, I was a chemist in my earlier life. But it doesn't require any great intelligence to become a chemist. Any common sense man can do it.

Mike Robinson: But presumably you think that material science is also important, even if today's scientists are dull-headed.

Śrīla Prabhupāda: Material science is important just so far. It is not all-important.

Mike Robinson: I see. Can I come back to a question I had from before? When we were differing a few minutes ago you were saying, "Don't bring the scriptures in; just use common sense." But what part do the scriptures play in your religion? How important are they?

Religion As Science

Śrīla Prabhupāda: Our religion is a science. When we say that a child grows into a boy, it is science. It is not religion. Every child grows into a boy. What is the question of religion? Every man dies. What is the question of religion? And when a man dies, the body becomes useless. What is the question of religion? It is science. Whether you're Christian or Hindu or Muslim, when you die your body becomes useless. This is science. When your relative dies, you cannot say, "We are Christian; we believe he has not died." No, he has died. Whether you are Christian or Hindu or Muslim, he has died. So when we speak, we speak on this basis: that the body is important only as long as the soul is in the body. When the soul is not there, it is useless. This science is applicable to everyone, and we are trying to educate people on this basis.

Mike Robinson: But if I understand you correctly, you seem to be educating people on a purely scientific basis. Where does religion come into it at all?

Śrīla Prabhupāda: Religion also means science. People have wrongly taken religion to mean faith—"I believe." [*To a devotee*] Look up the word religion in the dictionary.

Disciple: Under religion the dictionary says, "recognition of superhuman control or power, and especially of a personal

God entitled to obedience, and effecting such recognition with the proper mental attitude."

Śrīla Prabhupāda: Yes. Religion means learning how to obey the supreme controller. So, you may be Christian and I may be Hindu; it doesn't matter. We must both accept that there is a supreme controller. Everyone has to accept that; that is real religion. Not this "We believe animals have no soul." That is not religion. That is most unscientific. Religion means scientific understanding of the supreme controller: to understand the supreme controller and obey Him—that's all. In the state, the good citizen is he who understands the government and obeys the laws of the government, and the bad citizen is the one who doesn't care for the government. So, if you become a bad citizen by ignoring God's government, then you are irreligious. And if you are a good citizen, then you are religious.

Can Suffering Be Enjoyment?

Mike Robinson: I see. Can you tell me what you believe to be the meaning of life? Why do we exist in the first place?

Śrīla Prabhupāda: The meaning of life is to enjoy. But now you are on a false platform of life, and therefore you are suffering instead of enjoying. Everywhere we see the struggle for existence. Everyone is struggling, but what is their enjoyment in the end? They are simply suffering and dying. Therefore, although life means enjoyment, at the present moment your life is not enjoyment. But if you come to the real, spiritual platform of life, then you'll enjoy.

Mike Robinson: Can you explain to me, finally, some of the stages you go through in spiritual life? What are the spiritual stages a new devotee of Kṛṣṇa goes through?

Śrīla Prabhupāda: The first stage is that you are inquisitive. "So," you say, "what is this Kṛṣṇa consciousness movement? Let me study it." This is called *śraddhā,* or faith. This is the beginning. Then, if you are serious, you mix with those who are cultivating this knowledge. You try to understand how they are feeling. Then you'll feel, "Why not become one of them?" And when you become one of them, then all your misgivings soon go away. You become more faithful, and then you get a real taste for Kṛṣṇa consciousness. Why aren't these boys going to see the cinema? Why don't they eat meat or go to the nightclub? Because their taste has changed. They hate all these things now. In this way, you make progress. First faith, then association with devotees, then removal of all misgivings, then firm faith, then taste, then God realization, and then love of God, the perfection. That is first-class religion. Not some ritualistic ceremony of "I believe, you believe." That is not religion. That is cheating. Real religion means to develop your love for God. That is the perfection of religion.

Mike Robinson: Thank you very much for talking with me. It's been a pleasure talking to you.

Śrīla Prabhupāda: Hare Kṛṣṇa.

EPILOGUE

During his prolonged disappearance from public view (1975 to 1980), John Lennon's desire to become a better human being, his concern for human suffering, and his and Yoko's hopes for a better world, a world of peace, remained. On May 27, 1979, newspapers in New York, London, and Tokyo carried the following "Love Letter," paid for by John and Yoko:

> More and more we are starting to wish and pray.... When somebody is angry with us, we draw a halo around his or her head in our minds. Suddenly the person starts to look like an angel to us. This helps us to feel warm inside, and that all people who came to us are angels in disguise.... It's true we can do with a few miracles right now.... The future of the earth is up to all of us.... Remember, we are writing in the sky instead of on paper—that's our song. Lift your eyes and look up in the sky. There's our message.

Ultimately, John Lennon did not follow any one spiritual path (including Kṛṣṇa consciousness), but he inspired millions to develop the desire for self-inquiry, spiritual awareness, and the quest for world peace.

His tragic death shocked and angered the millions who loved and admired him. Yet John Lennon believed in *karma* and reincarnation. How could he die by such a senseless act of violence? Who can say? Surely the answer lies in the intricate and mysterious laws of *karma,* which operate far beyond the range of human perception.

Although the soul never dies, all great spiritual authorities throughout the ages have taught that until one becomes free from all material desires and attachments, one cannot achieve complete liberation from the cycle of birth and death. But whatever good one does, that *karma* follows him into his next life, and whatever true spiritual advancement one makes, that profit is eternal.

—The Publishers